THE CARVER POLICY GOVERNANCE® GUIDE SERIES

The *Carver Policy Governance® Guide* series includes six booklets that briefly describe John Carver's Policy Governance model of board leadership. Policy Governance is a precise job design for governing boards of equity, nonprofit, and governmental organizations. It enables boards to fulfill their accountability to the organization's "owners," whether owners are association members, city residents, company shareholders, or a community of interest.

The Policy Governance model is based on the functions rather than the structure of a governing board. It is primarily a set of commonsense principles about governing that fit together into an entire system. The practices of the Policy Governance board, which are consistent with the principles, allow it to control without meddling, focus on long-term organizational outputs, powerfully delegate to a CEO and staff, and discharge its fiduciary responsibility in a visionary, strategic manner. Because the model is a total system, it does not fulfill its promise when used piecemeal.

Policy Governance addresses the board's engagement in financial, programmatic, and personnel matters; roles of officers and committees; reporting and evaluation; agendas; and other aspects of the board job. A full, detailed explanation of Policy Governance can be found chiefly in John Carver's *Boards That Make a Difference*, 3rd edition, 2006, and in other publications as well (see inside back cover).

Policy Governance® is an internationally registered service mark of John Carver. Registration is only to ensure accurate description of the model rather than for financial gain. The model is available free to all with no royalties or license fees for its use. The authoritative Web site for Policy Governance is www.carvergovernance.com.

The Carver Policy Governance Guide Series

The Policy Governance Model and the Role
of the Board Member
A Carver Policy Governance Guide, Revised and Updated

Ends and the Ownership
A Carver Policy Governance Guide, Revised and Updated

The Governance of Financial Management
A Carver Policy Governance Guide, Revised and Updated

Adjacent Leadership Roles: CGO and CEO
A Carver Policy Governance Guide, Revised and Updated

Evaluating CEO and Board Performance
A Carver Policy Governance Guide, Revised and Updated

Implementing Policy Governance and Staying on Track
A Carver Policy Governance Guide, Revised and Updated

Praise for the Policy Governance Model

"Reading these guides is a great way to start your journey towards excellence in governance. All the essentials are there, short but clear. And these six guides will also prove to be an excellent GPS device along the way."

—Jan Maas, PG consultant, Harmelen, The Netherlands

"The guides are a great way to introduce busy board members to the basic principles of Policy Governance. Their bite-size approach is inviting, covering the entire model, albeit in less detail, without overwhelming the reader. They are succinct and easy to read, including practical points of application for board members. Consultants asked to recommend initial reading about the model can do no better than these guides."

—Jannice Moore, president, The Governance Coach™, Calgary, Canada

"Boards introduced to Policy Governance quickly become hungry for information but are short on time. These guides help board members quickly absorb the key principles of the Policy Governance model. They are invaluable."

—Sandy Brinsdon, governance consultant, Christchurch, New Zealand

"For some board leaders the governance elephant is best eaten one bite at a time. The Carver Policy Governance Guide series provides a well-seasoned morsel of understanding in a portion that is easily digested."

—Phil Graybeal, Ed.D., Graybeal and Associates, LLC, Greer, South Carolina

"Would you or your board benefit from a quick overview of essential governance concepts from the world's foremost experts on the topic, John and Miriam Carver? Thanks to their new six-booklet series, you can quickly familiarize or refresh yourself with the principles that make Policy Governance the most effective system of governance in existence. These booklets are the perfect solution for board members who are pressed for time but are dedicated to enhancing their own governance skills."

—Dr. Brian L. Carpenter, CEO, National Charter Schools Institute, United States

The POLICY GOVERNANCE MODEL

and the Role of the BOARD MEMBER

Revised and Updated

JOHN CARVER
MIRIAM CARVER

JB JOSSEY-BASS™
A Wiley Brand

Published by Jossey-Bass
A Wiley Imprint
989 Market Street, San Francisco, CA 94103-1741   www.josseybass.com

Jossey-Bass books and products are available through most bookstores. To contact Jossey-Bass directly call our Customer Care Department within the U.S. at 800-956-7739, outside the U.S. at 317-572-3986, or fax 317-572-4002.

Jossey-Bass also publishes its books in a variety of electronic formats. Some content that appears in print may not be available in electronic books.

Library of Congress Cataloging-in-Publication Data
Carver, John.
  The policy governance model and the role of the board member: a Carver policy governance guide / John Carver and Miriam Carver.—Rev. and updated ed.
     p. cm.—(The Carver policy governance guide series)
  ISBN 978-0-470-39252-2 (alk. paper)
  1. Boards of directors. 2. Corporate governance. I. Carver, Miriam Mayhew. II. Title.
  HD2745.C3726 2009
  658.4'22—dc22

                                                                           2009003153

Printed in the United States of America
REVISED AND UPDATED EDITION
HB Printing   SKY10065419_012224

If you serve on a board of directors, work for one, or observe one, you may have wondered whether there is any rhyme or reason to governance. You are not alone. Many have noticed characteristics of even good boards that are hard to explain.

Why, for example, do boards tend to spend hours debating small issues while large ones sail by comparatively unexamined? Why do groups of competent and assertive individuals allow themselves to be held hostage by the loudest or most insistent board member? Why do boards spend hours making decisions that they then forget they made or that go unrecorded or, if recorded, are difficult to locate? Why do boards, realizing the need to evaluate the performance of the organization they govern, try to perform such an evaluation in the absence of previously stated criteria? Why is the focus of boards on the present, or worse the past, instead of the future? Why do they seem more concerned about the activities of the organization than its outcomes? Why do boards approve reports of things that have already happened? And why don't they consider the consequences of not approving them? Why do they so often treat the chief executive officer (CEO) as either their friend or their enemy but rarely as their employee, to whom clarity and fairness but not subservience are owed? Why are boards of effective individuals so often ineffective groups? How can "model" boards, like Enron's was said to be, allow complete disaster? Why do current corporate governance writers complain that it still isn't clear what the role of a nonexecutive chair should be?

These and other questions commonly cause confusion and, in the end, ineffectiveness in governing boards. We are referring here to boards of all sorts: of nonprofit, for-profit, governmental, and co-operative organizations. You can get a clear answer to the question "What is your job" if you ask anyone in the organization *except the board*. Yet the board is accountable for the organization, its successes and its failures, and the board has more authority than any other part of the organization.

Imagine

It isn't difficult to imagine what excellent governance by boards should look like. Most people would agree with these ideals: boards should know who they work for; they should require their organizations to be effective and efficient; they should be in control of their organizations; the control they exercise should be of a type that empowers, not strangles; they should be fair in judging but unafraid to judge, rigorously holding delegatees accountable; they should be disciplined as to their role and their behavior; they should require discipline with regard to the role and behavior of their individual members; as the highest authority in enterprise, they should be predictable and trustworthy.

This is quite a vision for the governance of organizations, whether they be nonprofit, for-profit, or governmental. Yet as compelling as that vision is, in reality the process of governance is the least developed element in enterprise. It is, as you have no doubt noticed, a job that is ill-defined, undisciplined, dependent on staff rather than exercising leadership of them, and often actually irrelevant.

What accounts for the difference between the vision and the reality? Our answer focuses not on the skills or aspirations of the people who serve on boards but on their not using a governance system worthy of the importance of their job. Using a good governance methodology and first-rate discipline, boards can be visionary yet practical leadership bodies. The method and discipline of Policy Governance require much of board members to be sure, but what important job can you name that does not require a period of learning and ongoing discipline? We argue in the Carver Policy Governance Guides that achieving excellence in such an important leadership role is worth giving up some old practices, adopting some new ideas, and transforming the very nature of boardroom activity. The simple message is that boards can truly be effective leaders.

A Theory-Based Framework for Leadership and Accountability

Why is it important or even useful to base board practices in a governance theory? First, let us establish that by "theory," we don't mean head-in-the-clouds notions that are unrelated to the real world. We mean a carefully constructed set of ideas that completely cover a subject at a level deep enough to get underneath all the surface differences that are easier to see. In fact, theory is built by observing actual phenomena in enough places and under enough conditions that the underlying realities start showing themselves. Modern knowledge and capability had their greatest advances when someone worked out theories to replace trial-and-error or superstition. That is how people figured out gravity, germs, aerodynamics, and atoms. When sound theory becomes available, however, practices that seemed to make sense before are exposed as inadequate while practices no one had thought of before turn out to be essential. Until the Policy Governance model came along, governance had not yet benefited from such theory-building.

The Policy Governance model, created by John Carver, is a job design for boards, a prescription for leadership by any governing board in order to enable the quality of leadership of which boards are capable. It is a model in the conceptual rather than the structural sense, created to answer these questions: How does a group of equals, usually on behalf of someone else, direct an organization so that it is successful? How can it empower those who work in the organization as much as is safely possible, and how can it drive the organization toward the accomplishment of its long-term purpose? How can the board be crystal clear about what it should do and what should be left to others? And how can it be disciplined enough as a group to maintain a clear separation of function between its job and those of the people to whom it delegates? And what, when you get right down to it, is the difference between governance and management?

In order to answer these and other important questions, Policy Governance has a small number of principles or rules that, taken together, describe a complete operating system for boards. But you will find that these rules require the board to act very differently from what the traditional board is used to. Policy Governance is a new game and learning it poses challenges, especially for those used to the old one. One of the challenges you will have as a board member is the *system* nature of Policy Governance. Just as in a mechanical system, such as a clock, all the parts contribute to the functioning of other parts as well as to the total purpose. This is not unlike members of a sports team enhancing one another's performance as they all aim toward winning the contest. Removing just one cog from one wheel in an analog clock keeps it from telling time. Clocks, unlike governance, are products of careful design; typical board practices have not been designed so much as inherited. The strength in designed systems is their accuracy and power; the weakness is that they don't work if we pick and choose which parts to use and which to omit.

> So if you are a board member, it is important to be ready for new learning that can be counterintuitive until you master the ideas and practices. Policy Governance is an approach unlike anything that went before, even by the best of traditional boards. This can be a particular challenge if you have years of active board experience.

You may be aware that the reason for having a board at all is so that it can ensure accountability in and for the organization it governs. This means that the board occupies a special place between the organization's owners and the operating organization. The board is the agent of the owners and works for them, while the CEO is the agent of the board and works for it. Ownership is a concept that is very clear and even legally defined for some organizations. Shareholders own the company. Members own the trade association. Residents of a geographical area own city government and public school systems. But in nonprofit organizations without legal owners, it is useful to consider that they too are owned by persons outside the board, often a community or a community of interest. Policy Governance boards act consciously on behalf of owners and spend a considerable amount of time connecting to them and understanding their diversity.

So if you are a board member, you must make your decisions on behalf of the owners, not the staff, today's clients or recipients, or yourself. Morally, even if not legally, you and your board colleagues are agents of the owners.

It helps for boards to see themselves as active links in a chain of command, a chain of moral authority that connects owners to the organization they own. Policy Governance boards know that they are accountable to owners that the organization performs appropriately or, put more simply, that the operational organization works (a term we will define later). They understand that the board is the starting point of all authority in the parts of the organization that are normally visible to us (board and staff). We must recognize the owners, of course, as the true starting point, but boards as owners' agents are their on-site embodiment.

In this crucial, linking position, the responsible board adheres to a very strict rule that the authority of the board resides in the board as a body, not in members of the board. If you are on a nine-member board, you do not have one-ninth of the authority; you have none of it, while the board has all of it. We call this the one-voice principle, and not following it is a major reason for governance dysfunction. It requires the board, after sufficient debate, to reach a position that everyone may not have agreed with but that no one undermines. The one voice we mean is not the chair's voice but whatever the board as a group, using whatever voting method it has established, has decided.

So if you are a board member, you are obligated to support the legitimacy of board decisions that you disagree with, though there is no reason you should have to hide your disagreement.

This one-voice principle applies to all types of board decisions, whether about the board itself, its methods for connecting with owners, or instructions to the operational organization. That means that individual board members have no authority over staff, not even the authority to foist their help and advice, for that would fly in the face of board wholeness. This rule does not require board members to refrain from dissent, but does prevent their individual opinion from having the weight of authority. In other words, unless the board has spoken with one voice, it hasn't spoken at all. The board's message to its CEO, then, is that board members' ideas can be ignored but board decisions cannot be.

Except in the case of really small organizations, boards rely on others to do the actual work. In other words, they must delegate the running of the organization while remaining accountable for it. Consequently, accountable governance is very closely tied to accountable delegation. Accountable delegation requires the completion of three steps. First, the board must clearly set out its expectations of the job to be done or, put another way, the definition of success. Second, the board must identify who is expected to see that the board's expectations are met and assign to that person the authority that is needed to meet them. Third, the board must subsequently require evidence that its expectations were met. In this Guide, we will organize much of our description of the Policy Governance model around these three sequential elements in assuring accountability.

Setting Expectations by Type and Size

Because boards are accountable for their organizations, they set expectations in order to establish control over them. When Policy Governance boards set expectations, they use some specially designed principles and usually call their expectations "policies." We know that you are accustomed to hearing the word *policy* and that it means different things to different people. Traditionally, boards have always said they had policies, as well as other documents called "missions," "objectives," "goals," "strategies," "tactics," or "plans."

In Policy Governance, the word *policy* simply means written statements of what the board expects of itself or of those to whom it delegates. However, because the board is accountable for everything in the organization including its own functioning, its policies must be inclusive; they must leave nothing out. They must include all activities, decisions, outcomes, and circumstances of the organization. Not only must board policies be inclusive, they must be carefully formulated. You know as well as we do that it is possible to be in control in such a way that no one else has any room to move. When you have as much authority as a board has, it is very important to have policies that not only control but also empower the other people in the organization who have work to do. This can be a difficult balance to find.

> So if you are a board member, you must understand that as an individual, you have no authority over the organization and that no one who works in the organization works for you.

The Policy Governance board starts its work by acknowledging its need to control the entire organization and its own work. You would not have to spend too long thinking about the whole organization to realize that there are uncountable numbers of decisions and circumstances that occur every day in an organization. There are so many variables, in fact, that the board needs a way of organizing them in order to make its policies. The organizing approach in Policy Governance is based on two principles, one that deals with the *type of a decision* and one that deals with the *breadth of a decision*.

Ends and Means—Distinguishing the Prize from the Path

In Policy Governance, there are two basic types of decisions, *ends* and *means*. Here's how it works. Every organizational decision or action that describes the *effect to be produced* by the organization for an intended recipient outside the organization is an ends decision. Every designation of the *intended recipient of the effect* is an ends decision. Every designation of the *cost or priority of the effect* is an ends decision. Rather than saying "cost or priority," we will typically use the word *worth*, since it can refer both to the cost of results in monetary terms and to the "cost" of one result in terms of other results forgone. The former is an expectation about efficiency, the latter one about priority or opportunity cost, but in both cases the board is addressing the worth of recipients' results.

So if you are a board member, using words with either old or ambiguous definitions will damage communication with your colleagues. It isn't that words themselves matter, but that agreed upon definitions matter. That is always an important point, but even more so when considering making changes in concepts.

Consequently, ends decisions are *only* those that designate results, recipients, and worth of results. *All* other decisions are, naturally, *non-ends* decisions, but to use a less awkward term, we will call anything that is not an ends decision a *means* decision. Notice that ends decisions plus means decisions add up to all possible decisions.

Avoiding the Activity Trap

Describing the difference to be made in the lives of designated recipients and the worth of the various differences to be made is a robust way of describing an organization's purpose. It is robust because it describes organizational purpose not in terms of organizational activity (for example, a program, a service, or a curriculum) but in terms of the effect created on the world outside the organization. Ends expressed by a housing agency might be that economically disadvantaged people will have adequate and affordable places to live sufficient to justify the cost of providing them. Running a housing program, something the organization undoubtedly does, is not an ends issue. Ends expressed by a school system might be that young people will have skills and capabilities necessary for success, worth the taxes spent. Teaching a curriculum, something the school system is sure to do, is not an ends issue. Ends expressed by a listed equity corporation might be that shareholders receive a return on investment that is competitive with similar businesses with similar risk characteristics. Engaging in manufacturing or marketing, likely company activities, is not an ends issue. Ends, therefore, address what an organization is *for*, not what it *does*. Ends *never* describe organizational activity, no matter how impressive or necessary.

You might be noticing that describing ends is not something that boards commonly do. Boards spend huge amounts of time exploring, mandating, and criticizing activities but are often rather unclear about the reason for all the activities. The ends-means distinction focuses our attention on the fact that activities and results are not the same. The board that requires its organization to engage in activities will probably be satisfied when it does. The board that requires the *right results* for the *right people* at the *right worth* will not be satisfied with activities as these are not what it asked for.

So if you are a board member, the new concept of ends, despite its apparent simplicity, will take some getting used to. It isn't the same as goals, objectives, plans, or mission. Ends are simply the designation of organizational results, who gets the results, and the cost or priority of the results—with no "contamination" by methods used to achieve or support them.

Means include governance, finance, human resource issues, and all organizational actions including programs, services, and curricula. Governance itself is a uniquely board means, while all other means are operational. You may be surprised to see programs, services, and curricula listed as means. We are all accustomed to these activities being treated as ends in themselves. But they are only activities, even though they are important ones, and it is impossible to know if they are worthwhile unless they can be proven to accomplish the right results, for the right target populations, at the right worth.

Let's consider for a moment what the ends-means distinction is *not*. It is not based on a division of labor between board and staff, since in order to control all aspects of the entire organization, the board must make policies about means as well as ends. Further, it is not related to goals and objectives, policy and procedure, or strategy and tactics, since none of these more common terms respect the difference between the ends and means concepts as we've described them. (We are not questioning the utility of these terms in management, just in governance.) Also, the ends-means separation is not based on importance, since both ends and means are important.

The ends-means principle is a uniquely powerful key to designing responsible governance, though it is quite different from other ways of separating issues. It is a distinction that is a cornerstone of the Policy Governance model; you will not be able to use the model without learning it. We discuss ends in more detail in the Carver Policy Governance Guide *Ends and the Ownership.*

So if you are a board member, you must learn this very special way of separating organizational issues into two discrete categories. Just because an issue seems important or seems to you something the board should decide does not make it an ends issue. Keep going back to the definition until it becomes second nature.

Why is the ends-means distinction so important? First, making the distinction at all allows us to notice that ends tend to be hardly mentioned by boards while means seem to get a great deal of attention. That is an odd balance, since ends describe the externally focused purpose of the organization and means don't. Second, separating ends from means allows the board to control the two categories differently, in a way that gives management a great deal of room to move without giving away the shop.

Using the Ends-Means Distinction to Control and Empower

First, let's restate that everything the board is accountable for can be divided into ends and means—being careful to use their special Policy Governance meanings, not the usual dictionary definitions.

The means category is subdivided into board means and operational means. That is a useful further distinction, but it does not relieve the board from its accountability for either. The board remains accountable for everything and must control everything at some level. It must make policies about everything—and now we have three categories of issues that add up to "everything": ends, board means, and operational or staff means.

Writing Policies About Ends, Board Means, and Operational Means

As to *ends*, the board with a long-term perspective and with the input of owners and advisers, creates policies that prescribe what is to be produced, for whom, and at what worth. As to *board means*, the board creates policies that prescribe its own job and conduct. But as to *operational means*, the board, in order to optimally control the operating organization, creates policies with a peculiar but very important characteristic: these policies tell the CEO what *not* to do rather than what to do.

Typically, boards prescribe operational means largely through the tradition-blessed practice of board approvals. By approving staff actions or plans, the board has in effect decided what they should be; this has the effect of making them official or prescribing them. You have probably noticed that the prescriptions of operational means made by the board seldom originate with the board but are usually developed by staff. This is what we describe as the "tell us what to tell you" process.

There are a number of problems associated with boards prescribing operational means.

First, if the board prescribes the ends to be accomplished and wants to hold the CEO accountable for their accomplishment, telling the CEO how to do it causes a big problem. What if the board's means prescriptions don't work? Who is accountable for the failure to produce ends? What if they do work? Who is accountable for success? It is not fair to hold the CEO accountable for decisions made by the board, so prescribing the means has the effect of relieving the CEO of accountability or of imposing unfair blame.

Second, in order for the board to prescribe means well, it has to be as knowledgeable about running the organization as the CEO should be expected to be. Board members, of course, have their own skills, but to expect them to be qualified to be the CEO of the organization they govern is unrealistic and unnecessary.

Third, it has the effect of reducing management's ability to operate with agility, creativity, and responsiveness. If board approval is required for means decisions, management can manage only as responsively as the board can issue approvals. To tie full-time management decision making to a part-time board schedule seems inefficient. It is control, to be sure, and control that may reduce board anxiety, but it carries a high price.

Fourth, there is no logical need for the board to do all the work associated with prescribing operational means if what it is concerned about is that the organization use *effective* means. The board can easily find out if the organization used effective means: it simply has to find out if the ends were accomplished. This logic justifies a strong and, to some, a startling conclusion: as far as the effectiveness of operational means is concerned, there is no need for the board to be involved at all, whether to inspect, approve, or otherwise concern itself, particularly since such involvement threatens to reduce accountability rather than strengthen it.

> So if you are a board member with expertise or interest in some component of organizational means (such as human resources, accounting, or program planning), you must remember that indulging your interest is neither part of your board responsibility nor your authority, except as it might help you contribute to board debate about applicable policies.

But that doesn't mean the board has no legitimate interest in operational means. The board is as accountable for operational means as it is for everything else. But if the means are effective—that is, if they work—as demonstrated by ends achievement, what is there for the board to be worried about? Every board we've worked with agrees that even if operational means are effective, they could nonetheless be unacceptable. Unacceptable means are those that, even if effective, are imprudent, unlawful, or unethical. So the board's interest in operational means is not their effectiveness but their prudence and ethics. Policy Governance boards set expectations about operational means by describing what would be unacceptable to the board *even if effective*.

> So if you are a board member, remember you are on the board to govern, not manage. Using your area of expertise to draw your colleagues into setting prescriptive requirements for operational means is an inappropriate use of authority that allows the CEO to take no responsibility for operational means decisions that he or she did not make. The most you can responsibly do is make yourself available to the CEO on a strictly advisory basis, aware that "strictly advisory" means the CEO is under no obligation to take your advice.

Stating what is unacceptable does not draw the board into telling the CEO how the organization should be run, so the board does not need to know all the operational methods well enough to dictate them. Stating what is imprudent and unethical, on the other hand, is within the grasp of all conscientious board members. But more important than making life easier for some board members, this counterintuitive, unusual method of control has the effect of freeing the staff to be creative, responsive, and agile with respect to means. They can do whatever it takes to produce the board-required ends as long as they avoid board-prohibited means.

Freedom Within Boundaries

The effect of telling the CEO what not to do, rather than what to do, is that the board makes policies that are negative instead of positive; that is, they are proscriptive, not prescriptive. We call this category of board policies *Executive Limitations* because they spell out the limits placed on executive authority. They spell out *all* the limits; that is, they are comprehensive, leaving nothing out. With such thorough Executive Limitations policies in place, the board can responsibly say that operational means not placed out of bounds are, by definition, within the CEO's authority.

In a way, this is a preapproval system that eliminates the need for the board to be involved in ongoing operational decision making. Board approvals of the familiar sort, in which the board examines an operational plan in order to give it the board's blessing, no longer occur. Policy Governance boards engage in no approvals of operational issues except those required by outside parties such as regulators, funders, or accrediting agencies. Even those required approvals—as we explain in the Carver Policy Governance Guide *Implementing Policy Governance and Staying on Track*—are dealt with in a way designed to avoid breaking down the powerful delegation system Policy Governance enables.

Board policies worded in a "don't let this occur" fashion may feel quite unnatural and sometimes even verbally awkward. Yet many matters of law or other regulation are in this form. We are not normally told how fast to drive, but how fast *not* to drive. We are not told what date to file our tax return, but the date after which we must pay a penalty. We may not tell our son or daughter when to mow the lawn, but when will constitute doing it too late. Still, you may feel quite uncomfortable and a sense of negativity when you see an accumulation, all in one place, of negatively worded policies. You may worry that the negative wording sounds so, well, negative. But keep in mind that only one category of board policies in Policy Governance has this characteristic. The negative wording is useful for two reasons.

One reason is to prevent boards' almost irresistible tendency to apply their considerable wisdom, real or imagined, to telling subordinates how to do their jobs. You have probably seen for yourself how strong this tendency is, especially if the board is composed of persons greatly skilled or experienced in staff roles and perhaps less comfortable with the enterprise of governing. It is hard not to be motivated to do what one knows best. Using the negative language is a constant reminder to boards and their members that prescription of operational means is to be avoided at all costs.

Another reason is that even though the words themselves are negative, the psychological effect of using this sort of control is very positive for the CEO. He or she is being told that as long as disallowed means are avoided, any means decision he or she makes is authorized by the board. This is welcomed by CEOs who have seen their peers lose their jobs for making decisions only later described as unacceptable. And, in the face of changing conditions, it is appreciated by CEOs whose ability to respond decisively and quickly is limited by needing to bring board members up to date so they can study, deliberate, and finally decide to approve. Because it is sometimes hard to do that in a timely manner, opportunities can be lost.

We need to add a caution that boards can misuse proscriptive language to prescribe means, so great is the tendency to prescribe. Such "back door" prescriptions often take the form of "the CEO shall not fail to have [or operate without]" some specified means, for example, "The CEO shall not fail to select instructional materials that integrate the curriculum by course and program" or "The CEO shall not fail to use the Balanced Scorecard management approach." These are obviously prescriptions of means despite their verbal format. Proper Executive Limitations prohibit means that are not acceptable *even if they work*. These examples fail that test, for a board's pleasure over achievement of its Ends policies would not be diminished because the CEO used a different method. Contrast an Executive Limitations policy that passes the test: "The CEO shall not subject staff to dangerous work conditions." That prohibition stands on its own ethics and prudence rationale, so that one can mentally add, "even if all other Executive Limitations and Ends policies are fulfilled."

So if you are a board member, you must discipline your natural instincts to prescribe means and help your colleagues on the board do likewise. If it seems a little against human nature to stay proscriptive, not prescriptive in the operational means category, remember all our other capabilities that once seemed out of reach. Think of flight, gymnastics, and Sudoku . . .

The Board's Job—Prescribing Ends
and Prohibiting Unacceptable Means

The board's job, then, with regard to defining the organization's functioning, is to prescribe ends and to prohibit unacceptable means. When earlier we said the board is accountable to owners that the operational organization works, this is what "works" means: any organization can be said to work if it accomplishes the ends the board wanted and avoids the means that the board didn't want.

Defining the board's job this way is intended to ensure that the board maintains a proper distance from operational issues, a distance that is troublesome to board members who have been taught by tradition that being involved in staff work is a virtue. Although the Policy Governance model is open to individual board members' being as operationally involved as the CEO permits, it clearly calls for boards *as boards* to steer clear of such involvement. The concreteness and immediacy of operational means make them very attractive to many board members, so much so that boards sacrifice the independence they need to make fair judgments of performance on behalf of the owners. Boards of all sorts lose their independence by thinking their role should be advisory to staff. Equity corporate boards lose their independence in an additional way, by including executives on the board and, worse, even combining chair and CEO roles in one person.

> So if you are a board member, it may help to think of the board as a commander, not an adviser. It doesn't exist to help but to be in charge. The board's job, by no means an easy one: Set challenging expectations. Then get out of the way, except to check that they're accomplished.

In both instances, boards tend to recruit members based on the skills they have in one operational means area or another, so it is understandable that those members expect that these are the skills they should bring to the board table. Corporate boards try to include executives with skills in strategy, marketing, or production. Nonprofit boards are more likely to include personnel or accounting skills and experts in whatever is the subject matter of the organization (such as a psychiatrist on a mental health board). But as you have seen, a board using Policy Governance demands that its members not act as staff one step removed but rather to be part of a group that authoritatively defines the guiding values of the organization. The board acts not so much *in* the organization as *on* it. Thus, the board's job is not so much management one step up as ownership one step down and, therefore, requires the capabilities that fit that role.

There is, however, another difficulty to overcome about comprehensively limiting executive means. You may be wondering how the board can possibly remember all the ways in which operational decisions and situations might violate the board's sense of prudence and ethics. Since the message from board to CEO with regard to means is "if we haven't said you shall not, you may," how can the board avoid leaving out constraints it may later fervently wish it had remembered? In fact, other policy areas as well as Executive Limitations present a similar question, although admittedly one less frightening. For example, how can a board be sure it has covered everything it wishes in its Ends policies? In fact, how can a board be sure it has covered everything in its policies dealing with the board's own job?

These are legitimate questions. While the Policy Governance framework of ends and means enables many governance flaws to be overcome, another principle is needed to eliminate the possibility of policy incompleteness. Let us now, then, turn to how boards, in expressing each of the policy types, can address the matter of thoroughness.

Decisions Inside Decisions—
Distinguishing Decisions by Breadth

All policies, in fact all sentences, because they are formed from words, are open to interpretation. An Ends policy that requires a trade association CEO to produce "conditions conducive to the business success of members" sets an expectation, but it is open to considerable interpretation. Which members? All of them or the more established ones? Success at what: office management, public relations, accounting? What conditions: public image, helpful legislation, or regulation? An Ends policy that requires a corporate CEO to achieve "earnings per share comparable to similar companies" also sets an expectation open to further interpretation: similar in what regard—alike in capitalization, in type of market, in current market share? And how "similar" is similar enough? Likewise, an Executive Limitations policy that states that the CEO "will not allow anything in the operational organization to be unlawful, imprudent, or unethical" is open to interpretation. As people we frequently disagree about exactly what the words *unlawful, imprudent*, or *unethical* mean. Of course, all these words have to be further defined by someone, but exactly which someone? Who should be allowed to make these further decisions?

There is an organized way to answer that question. The solution is found in the Policy Governance principle of *sequential logical containment*. Informally, we usually refer to this as the "mixing bowl" principle. If you imagine a nested set of bowls (or cardboard boxes or Russian dolls), you can see that it is possible to control the entire set by having hands-on control of just the largest member of the set. All other members of the set are under control, even though they can move around within the confines of the larger items. You can also see that extending hands-on control further, bowl by bowl into the set, reduces the amount each of the interior bowls can move around. At some point, you will decide that the reduced range of motion of the smaller bowls is not something you are concerned about; it is at that point that, in your opinion, you have exerted sufficient control, even though it is not, and need not be, total control. You see this idea depicted in Figure 1.

Likewise, statements of policy can come in sizes, and the range that bowls have to move around in we can now call the *range of reasonable interpretation*. To say that the CEO will not allow anything

Figure 1. Hands-On, Hands-Off Control.

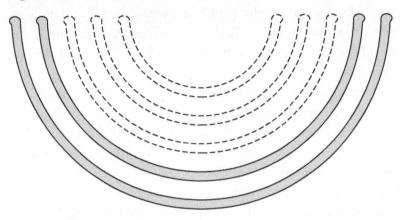

Note: Direct control of the outer bowls in a nested set allows indirect control of the smaller bowls. A board will decide to have hands-on control over the largest issues (depicted here by bowls drawn with a solid line) but indirect, hands-off control of smaller issues (depicted by bowls drawn with a broken line).

in the organization under his or her authority to be imprudent or un-ethical is clearly an Executive Limitations policy of the broad or "large bowl" size. To say that organizational assets should not be in-adequately maintained, unnecessarily risked, or unprotected is a smaller-bowl or narrower policy that provides one interpretation of *imprudent* but is itself still open to interpretation. To say that the or-ganization exists so that families can know how to resolve strife with-out violence is a large-bowl or broad Ends policy, while saying that priority will be given to families with small children is a smaller-bowl or narrower policy that further defines the broader Ends statement. Descending breadth means the same as increasing detail.

It is important to note that this process is unending, since any further definition just leads to the next smaller range of interpreta-tion. The board does not have the option of defining until no range is left, any more than we can define a cup of coffee in so much detail that there would be no further detail left. Even if a board could do that, doing so would be most unwise because the board would not be taking advantage of a whole staff of intelligent people. That would not be making the most of expensive human capital and would in effect amount to cheating the ownership. Of course, if the board really can remove all further ranges of decisions, it doesn't need a staff anyway!

Further, as a matter of decision making in general, all decisions by anyone can be viewed in this descending-breadth manner, whether in buying a personal car or choosing a college. Policy Governance simply takes this phenomenon of description and uses it, along with the ends-means principle, to handily separate decision authority that the board retains from that which it delegates.

So if you are a board member, think of decisions inside decisions inside decisions all the way from the broadest decision the board might make to the narrowest one made by the most organizationally distant staff member. Each of his or her decisions is wrapped in one above and that in another above until finally they are all inside the largest "wrapper" decided by the board.

Knowing that policies come in sizes, that is, that they can be stated broadly or narrowly, allows the board to take control just as surely as we do when picking up a set of bowls. But to do so, the board must first make the broadest, most inclusive decision of each topic. Only then can the board further define its words until the range of remaining interpretation has been reduced to the point that the board is able to accept any reasonable interpretation by someone else. At this point, it is finally safe for the board to delegate the right to someone to make any reasonable interpretation of the completed total policy. With respect to Ends and Executive Limitations policies, the CEO is given this authority, meaning that he or she is authorized to make interpretations and change them as necessary, as long as in every case his or her interpretations can be proven to the board to be reasonable. The disclosure and justification of CEO interpretations form a necessary part of monitoring reports, as we will discuss later in this Guide and also in the Carver Policy Governance Guide *Evaluating CEO and Board Performance*.

One reason boards need to approach decision making in this way is that the staff makes interpretations of the board's values anyway. You cannot carry out an instruction unless you interpret it. Even if the board retained the right to make every decision, there is no way staff can bring all choices to the board. Most boards would not even want them to. It is true that when a board approves a staff recommendation, it uses the values of board members to do so. After all, there is no basis for approval or disapproval but one's values. But even though board members' values are used, approval actions leave board values unclear. They are unclear because, first, the board members

So if you are a board member, it is important that you consider the range of interpretation made available by board policies and remember that "any reasonable interpretation" means just that. The CEO is not required to interpret a policy in the way you may have interpreted it. He or she is simply required to make (and accomplish) a reasonable interpretation. If you are not sure that a policy is defined enough to delegate to the CEO, you should feel free to press your colleagues for further policy extension. Once delegated, however, you are duty-bound to support any CEO interpretation that can be shown to the board's satisfaction, not just your own, to be reasonable.

probably did not state their values so much as their disagreement with some part of a document and, second, because the board didn't vote on the specific values, but on the total document. For example, if a budget has been approved, what values made it approvable and what values would have made it unapprovable?

Such questions remain unanswered no matter how much discussion occurs unless the board consciously makes decisions in a pattern that comes close to the process we've described. As a result, anyone, whether staff or board, who tries to determine with certainty what the board's values are will run into a patchwork of values that conflict with each other or are just impossible to figure out. Policy Governance eliminates that patchwork of governing values because the board expresses its values directly, not hidden in approvals or other discussions. It then, in recognition that all its expressions are

open to interpretation, carefully increases the detail until more detail isn't necessary at the board level. In that way, the Policy Governance board harnesses what can be a troublesome aspect of
human communication to produce more values-focused governance
and a clearer line where board decision making stops and staff decision making begins.

Board Policies Embrace the Organization

The Policy Governance board makes policies in this "mixing bowl"
manner about Ends and Executive Limitations on operational
means. These two policy sets constitute *all* the board's instruction
to the CEO. When considered along with board policies about
board means and the fact that all board policies are written in the
mixing-bowl manner, it can be said that the board, through these
policies, has its arms not only around all components of the organization but around all possible aspects of those components.

As to the board's policies about its own means, these are normally divided into two categories. First, *Governance Process policies*
describe the board's job, its connection with owners, and its expectations about the performance of itself, its chair, its committees, and
its members. Second, *Board-Management Delegation policies* describe
the manner in which the board connects governance to management. It is in this latter category where one can find the board's decisions to use a CEO function, to monitor that CEO's performance
in a defined way, and to establish CEO authority.

Even though the term CEO (for *chief executive officer*) is widely
used and understood at least in a general way, we should explain
what we mean by it. We mean the first position with executive authority below the full board. By "below" we mean that the position
receives its authority from and is directly accountable to the board.
In these Guides, we will frequently speak of the staff, meaning the
operational organization, and even more frequently speak of the
CEO. To a great extent, the terms *staff* and *CEO* are synonymous
insofar as the board telling the CEO what to accomplish means the

board is telling the CEO what the operational organization is to accomplish. Similarly, when the board holds the CEO accountable, it is really considering the accountability for the entire operational organization. If, for example, in an Executive Limitations policy, the board says the CEO "shall not cheat vendors," it doesn't mean just the CEO but the CEO and everyone over whom the CEO has authority—that is, the entire operational organization.

In Figure 2, we arrange these four categories of board policies as quadrants of a circle, showing the largest or broadest policy in

Figure 2. Decisions Arranged by Type and Breadth.

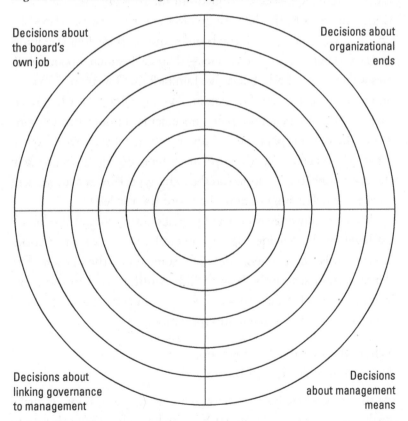

Note: The four categories of organizational decisions are shown as four sets of bowls, brought together to form four quadrants of a circle. Larger and smaller issues within those categories are shown as larger and smaller bowls.

each quadrant on the outside edge and, just like the bowls, smaller or narrower ones at various levels within the circle. We will use this circle diagram from now on to illustrate the entire set of a board's policies, along with the decision areas left to others under those policies.

In this graphic, the circle encloses all activities, decisions, outcomes, situations, and commitments of the entire organization—both board and staff. The four quadrants represent the four categories of board policies with their mixing-bowl sets turned upon one another to create the circle. This way, the largest bowl of each set is on the circumference, followed internally by smaller bowls in sequence all the way to the very tiniest decisions in the middle of the circle. On the right side, you see a quadrant for ends and one for operational means. On the left are quadrants for the two parts of the board's own means. When the board addresses these four quadrants at the broadest levels, as we've discussed, its deliberation produces policies we refer to as Ends, Executive Limitations, Governance Process, and Board-Management Delegation. (We capitalize *Ends* when referring to a board's actual Ends policy documents but not when referring to the idea or concept of ends.) Although the graphic shows the quadrants to be equal in size, there are many more decisions occurring in the operational organization (on the right, especially in management or operational means) than in the board (on the left).

In Figure 3, we see that board policies always start at the broadest level on the outside edge of the circle, but move into various "lower bowls," that is, more detail for some topics than others. The depth varies because the board will be willing to control some issues more loosely than others. "Loosely," of course, means to leave a larger range of reasonable interpretation.

Where the Board's Policies Stop, Delegation of Authority Begins

At the point where board policymaking stops, the authority to make further decisions is delegated. Only the board has the authority to decide where that point will be. There is not a "right" dividing line for all boards where board decision making should stop and CEO

Figure 3. The Policy Circle.

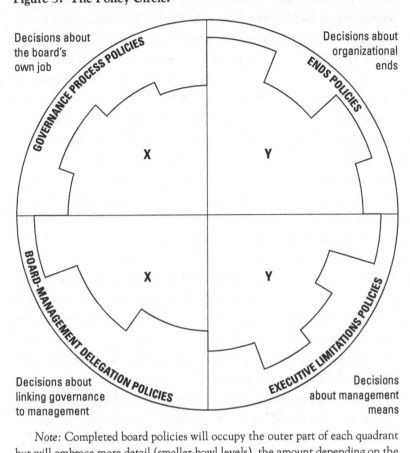

Note: Completed board policies will occupy the outer part of each quadrant but will embrace more detail (smaller-bowl levels), the amount depending on the board's values. The board will go into more detail about some policy topics than others, even within a given quadrant. Notice that the quadrant containing all staff means issues will be addressed by the board in a constraining or negative fashion (hence the policy category titled "Executive Limitations"). Empty space in the middle represents smaller decisions that the board is content to leave to delegatees. The CGO will be given authority to make decisions in the spaces marked X. (Foreshadowing later discussion of this role, CGO is used to indicate the chief governance officer, a function normally fulfilled by the board chair.) The CEO will be given authority to make decisions in the space marked Y.

decision making start. But for any particular organization, that dividing line should be crystal clear. In Policy Governance, it is easy to tell where the board's decision making has stopped, for its policies are written in a policy manual that is kept scrupulously up-to-date. A policy manual put together in this very special way is the board's focal point in Policy Governance, for no one knows what a group has said, even the group itself, if its statements are unwritten or difficult to locate.

> So if you are a board member, you need go to only one place to find everything the board has decided that is still in effect: the current board policy manual. It should always be up-to-date, accurate, and easily accessible.

On the right-hand side of the circle in Figure 3, the recipient of the delegated authority to make the rest of the decisions is the CEO. He or she is accountable to the board that the organization accomplishes a reasonable interpretation of the board's Ends policies while avoiding unacceptable means described by the board in Executive Limitations policies, reasonably interpreted. On the left side of the circle, the delegatee is the chief governance officer (CGO), an officer who is usually the chair of the board but whose job responsibilities include much more than chairing meetings. The CGO's job is to see to it that the board governs as it said it would govern in its Governance Process and Board-Management Delegation policies; the CGO is granted authority by the board to use any reasonable interpretation of those policies.

Board Policies Precede and Are Separate from All Other Decisions and Documents

You can see from Figure 3 that the board has made policies that cover everything in the organization, but it has done so by addressing the broader levels of all issues, not all the specifics. The more detailed levels are for the CEO or CGO to decide or to delegate further, subject to the requirement that the decisions made are reasonable interpretations of board policy. Let us reiterate that the board's policies in the four quadrants of the circle are *all* the board has to say. (We discuss the exception of bylaws in the Carver Policy Governance

Guide titled *Implementing Policy Governance and Staying on Track.*) There are no additional board documents, though staff will have many of their own documents for internal purposes.

This means that the organization's budget, strategic plan, and other documents commonly embraced by the board are really management's documents. They are components in the manager's arsenal of means to ensure organizational compliance with board policies. For example, with the exception of planning governance itself, organizational planning and budgeting are done and revised as necessary by staff, subject to applicable Executive Limitations policies. Because we recognize that this is an unusual way for boards to control important means like budgeting and risk management, we devote further discussion to the rationale and methods of financial governance in the Carver Policy Governance Guide titled *The Governance of Financial Management.*

Here are a few examples of policies in each category at the very top level. Three examples of Ends policies are shown because they differ so much from one organization to another.

> So if you are a board member, although the organization may have many documents, all documents except board policies and bylaws, if applicable, belong to the CEO. Although CEO documents are available to you as matters of personal interest, your responsibility is carried out entirely by adjustments of your powerful control "handles": prescriptive Ends policies and proscriptive Executive Limitations policies, each written to the detail that represents the board's "any reasonable interpretation" judgment.

Ends

"XYZ Trade Association members will enjoy conditions favorable for business success sufficient to justify their dues."

"People with developmental challenges will achieve their potential at a level justifying available resources."

"The three-year rolling average of earnings per share will be greater than the mean of similar organizations."

Executive Limitations

"The CEO shall not cause or allow conditions, activities, or decisions that are imprudent, unlawful, or in violation of customary business and professional ethics."

Governance Process

"The board, on behalf of the Jefferson community, exists to ensure that the Jefferson Historical Society is effective, prudent, and ethical."

Board-Management Delegation

"The board links governance and management through a single chief executive officer, titled *general manager*."

Although a board has the right to stop at this broad level, in fact few would, simply because they would not be willing to leave so broad a range of decision making to subordinate decision makers. Consequently, lower-level policies would say more about, for example, which business success, which developmentally compromised people, organizations similar in what respects, which ethical codes, how the board "ensures" achievement, and what is meant by "links" with management. At any rate, at some point, all boards will stop and leave it to others to make the remaining decisions.

You will see that both the CGO and the CEO are empowered to make decisions, but in separate domains. The roles of CGO and CEO are adjacent, and neither reports to the other. (We discuss these roles in more detail in the Carver Policy Governance Guide titled *Adjacent Leadership Roles: CGO and CEO*.) The CGO has no authority on the right side of the circle, and the CEO has none on the left. This means that like all other board members, the CGO has no executive authority. It also means that it is never the CEO's responsibility to make Governance Process decisions, such as what the board's agenda should be, for this would be giving the board's employee or subordinate the responsibility to see that his or her boss is responsible.

A Policy Governance board understands that if it cannot govern itself, it can hardly govern an organization, so it takes control of its own agenda. The board's agenda is developed from the board's overall job description, which describes the results, outputs, or "values added" that good governance should produce. Those results constitute an output type of job description rather than a list of activities. Creating a results-based job description of this sort requires a governance theory that describes what a board is for to begin with. The board's job description, like all board decisions, is put into the form of policy and, in this case, becomes part of the Governance Process category. The board using Policy Governance must produce three nondelegable outcomes—connection with owners, written governing policies, and assured organizational performance—all of which we discuss in greater detail in the Carver Policy Governance Guide titled *Implementing Policy Governance and Staying on Track*. These outputs when produced by the board allow it to ensure the translation of owner needs into organizational performance.

The three outputs are the irreducible minimum results to be produced by the board itself, but some boards choose to commit themselves to additional outcomes. A common example in nonprofit organizations is donor funding. This is a board job outcome if it is not delegated to the CEO. Interestingly, there are no job products shared between the board and the CEO. If there were, who would be accountable for their production, board or staff? Accountability is more effective and more easily traced if definable portions of a total job are assigned to separate actors rather than the total job to both.

Earlier we listed three steps in accountable delegation: first, setting expectations for performance; second, identifying delegatees; and third, inspecting evidence that expectations were met. At this point, we have discussed the first of these three steps in the delegation sequence: the board's manner of establishing its expectations, using the ends-means principle and the principle of sequential levels of detail. In making our point, we have occasionally mentioned the assignment of those expectations. Now we will focus directly on the second of the three steps in the delegation sequence: assigning board expectations and the authority to meet them.

Assigning Expectations and Authority Without Duplication

There is little point for the board to describe its expectations carefully if it is then unclear about who is accountable that the expectations are met. The board may delegate to committees and to individual board members, but its most common delegation inside the board itself is to the CGO. The most common delegation outside the board is to the CEO. That is, to help ensure the board's accountability is fulfilled, the board shares *parts* of the job of governance itself with committees and officers and gives the *entire* job of running the organization to the CEO. These delegated parts should never be allowed to overlap. To do so reduces the certainty of achievement, leaving the board's own accountability at risk—a precept expressed by the old management maxim "If two persons are responsible, no one is." Having shared out parts of its overall accountability, the board is still accountable for the total.

As shown in the right side of Figure 3, all authority for interpreting Ends and Executive Limitations policies is given to the CEO, along with accountability for their achievement. It is important that the CEO's authority over the operational organization be total; otherwise, the various divisions of effort that occur in management might not add up to success.

Similarly, as shown on the left side of Figure 3, all authority for interpreting Governance Process and Board-Management Delegation policies is given to the CGO, along with accountability for their achievement. A board can delegate portions of the left side to committees if it chooses, but the CGO remains the "default setting."

We recommend maintaining as much simplicity as possible, so that in this Guide we will only address the CEO and CGO as nonoverlapping delegatees. We will talk about committees too, but only to point out practices to avoid.

The CEO

When a board chooses to use a CEO function to connect the board to management, it has in effect decided that the job of making the organization work is delegated to the CEO and to the CEO alone. Ends and Executive Limitations policies are directions to the CEO— and only the CEO—and describe the board's expectations for organizational performance. If the board delegates the same job, or parts of it, to more than one person or group, it is unintentionally asking for the development of turf battles and enabling everyone except the board itself to evade accountability. The CEO function is useful precisely because it enables the board to focus its expectations on the organization as a whole rather than on the various divisions of labor within the organization. With Policy Governance, the internal divisions—the organizational chart of departments, offices, or other components—are means choices of the CEO. But the great utility for boards in having a CEO will exist only if the CEO function is correctly used.

In Figure 4, we see a very simple organizational chart or chain of command. The board works for the owners, so when it makes policies, particularly Ends policies, it does so on owners' behalf. In the diagram, there is a single arrow from the board to the CEO. This arrow represents the board's single voice, a voice that describes the organization's job, expressed in Ends and Executive Limitations policies. If there were more than one line to the CEO, to whose voice should the CEO listen and report? The board's? The loudest or most expert individual? The CEO's favorites? If the CEO is to comply with board expectations, then surely it only introduces confusion as well as a place to hide if the board allows others to instruct as well.

Figure 4. The Chain of Command from Ownership to CEO.

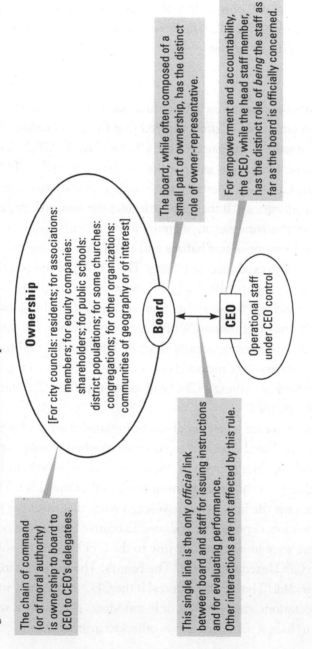

The board, while often composed of a small part of ownership, has the distinct role of owner-representative.

For empowerment and accountability, the CEO, while the head staff member, has the distinct role of *being* the staff as far as the board is officially concerned.

Ownership

[For city councils: residents; for associations: members; for equity companies: shareholders; for public schools: district populations; for some churches: congregations; for other organizations: communities of geography or of interest]

Board

CEO

Operational staff under CEO control

The chain of command (or of moral authority) is ownership to board to CEO to CEO's delegatees.

This single line is the only *official* link between board and staff for issuing instructions and for evaluating performance. Other interactions are not affected by this rule.

To the board, *officially* the CEO is the entire operational organization.
To the CEO, *officially* the board is the ownership in microcosm.

The Policy Governance board ensures that nothing in its structural arrangements interferes with its delegation to the CEO or comes between it and the CEO. Much of the power in proper delegation is its simplicity, a virtue easily sacrificed by clutter. Maintaining simplicity enables delegation to be both powerful and safe. If you think that the Policy Governance model gives a great deal of authority to the CEO, you are right. The CEO position is the board's device to ensure that the board's accountability to owners for an organization that works is fulfilled. To have a CEO and not empower him or her to the maximum is self-defeating.

The Policy Governance model can be used by a board that does not have a CEO. Governing without a CEO is more complex due to there being no focal point of empowerment and accountability. Consequently, since the use of Policy Governance must take these extra difficulties into account, we will not deal with them in these Guides.

The CGO

The chief governance officer, as depicted in Figure 3, is neither superior nor subordinate to the CEO. CGO and CEO are parallel offices, each empowered by and accountable to the board directly. Just as the board, to use Robert Greenleaf's term, is a servant-leader for the ownership, the CGO is a servant-leader for the board. That is, the CGO is not the board's boss but does have board-granted authority to interpret and enforce rules the board has set for itself. The board, in which all organizational authority resides at the outset, is composed of equals, none of whom has any authority as individuals. The board decides to take a defined amount of its group authority and give it to its "first among equals" in order to ensure the group discipline to which it is committed.

In other words, the CGO has only the authority the board decides. He or she is expected to perform so that a reasonable interpretation of the board's Governance Process and Board-Management Delegation policies is accomplished by the board. The CGO's authority and responsibility can be changed by the board at any time;

they are not for the CGO to decide. Servant-leadership of this sort is a sensitive balance to maintain, so deserves continual explicit attention by the board.

The CGO role is usually fulfilled by the person most boards call chair and some call president, but it is possible that a given CGO will discharge his or her obligation for policy-consistent meeting conduct by appointing a chair to carry out that part of the CGO's accountability. As with all delegation, the CGO remains accountable even if he or she has further delegated parts of the job.

We give more attention to the CEO and CGO roles in the Carver Policy Governance Guide titled *Adjacent Leadership Roles: CGO and CEO.*

Sources of Confused Accountability

In order to keep the board-to-CEO part of the chain of command diagrammed in Figure 4 intact, the board must take steps to avoid some common structural problems. There are a number of ways in which boards endanger their one voice and let the CEO off the hook of accountability. Here are some:

The Renegade Board Member

We regard board members as acting in a renegade way when they contradict or add to instructions given by the board to the CEO. Board members, often well-meaning, who give instructions to the CEO or other staff are interrupting the chain of command, thereby doing damage to the board's one voice and jeopardizing accountability. There is little the CEO or staff can do about this, but the board can fix the problem easily. The board must simply make clear that the CEO is only to be held accountable for meeting board expectations and never board member expectations. It must state and be consistent in its actions that CEO or organizational evaluation will never take place against criteria set by board members but only against criteria set by the board as a whole. This allows board members as individuals and staff members to interact as peers, ensuring that board members are never treated as authoritative. Of course, nothing prevents the CEO from asking for input from individuals on the board if he or she wishes. But board members foisting themselves into management clouds the issue of just who the CEO reports to.

The CGO or Chair

The CGO or chair is an important officer in the Policy Governance system, but he or she does not hold executive authority. We have often seen bylaws that describe the chair as the board member who has responsibility for the running of the organization, for the supervision of those running it, or for being the communication link between board and CEO. We have seen chairs decide on their own to give instructions to the organization, usually because the board has not done so itself. Such roles for a board chair damage accountability. Policy Governance boards eliminate wording from their bylaws that gives the chair the right to be, as it were, the über-CEO, since the chair with such authority diminishes the accountability of the intended CEO. It does so by risking turf battles over authority and by obscuring who is accountable for performance. And Policy Governance boards require their CGOs to press the board itself to set expectations for the CEO, for that is what the board will have agreed to in its own job description.

The Treasurer or Finance Chair

It is easy to understand that in a very small organization without staff or one with staff but no CEO, asking a financially skilled board member to look after the books makes a good deal of sense. However, when the organization has a CEO, it is this officer and not the treasurer who must be held accountable for financial management. Bylaws that describe the treasurer as accountable to the board that finances are handled prudently should be changed. A CEO not empowered to make and be held accountable for financial decisions is not really a CEO at all. If your organization is required by law or regulation to have a treasurer who is a board member, the job should be described in a way that enhances the board's ability to govern rather than interferes with delegation to the CEO. For example, if permissible, the board can describe its treasurer as responsible for the board's being well enough informed to create sound policies about finances. Those policies then become incumbent on the CEO, not the treasurer, to fulfill.

Board Committees in General

Committee-like forms are often known by other names, such as task force. But no matter what alternate term is used, the same rules apply. Therefore, the Policy Governance rules for committees apply to any group that is created by the board or is given its job by the board, no matter who is in it or what it is called. When committees are created to help the board carry out its own hands-on job, they can be very useful. But many board committees are created in order to instruct, help, or advise staff. If the CEO is to be held accountable by the board for meeting its expectations, those expectations or instructions should come only from the board, not from committees. Other involvement can honestly be called help or advice only if the input provided was invited by the CEO and can be ignored by him or her. Input that cannot be ignored is instruction. You are well aware that staff members normally do not feel free to ignore the input of board committees, even when the committees genuinely intend only to be advisory. Committees of the board necessarily interrupt the chain of command when given jobs to do in the staff domain. This is why Policy Governance boards observe the rule that they will create committees to help with governance but will not create them to help with management. The CEO can create all the committees he or she wants, but they would not be board committees. This is a simple rule, but it ensures that the board-CEO relationship remains uncluttered and unambiguous and that the CEO remains fully accountable for operational decisions made.

The Executive Committee

Executive committees are often created by bylaws to ensure that someone has authority "in case something
comes up between board meetings."
Of course, between board meetings is
when things *do* come up, and to have
no delegatees clearly empowered to
make decisions makes no sense. Policy Governance boards give their
CEO and CGO sufficient authority
over their domains, making an executive committee rarely necessary.
Often an executive committee with

So if you are a board member,
resist the temptation to suggest
or support the creation of officer
or committee roles that overlap
with the job given to the CEO.
If you want to volunteer to help
out in operations, the decision
whether you can do so belongs
to the CEO. This volunteer help,
even if accepted, is not a board
activity but an individual one.
The board, as a board, exists to
govern, not to help out.

the authority to make decisions when the board is not in session
may actually be the board more than the board is the board. That
is a huge power giveaway, made especially suspect since that authority is almost never accompanied by performance expectations.
In addition, executive committees are smaller and more agile than
the entire board and can process a large number of decisions into
which the board has little or no input. Board members not on the
executive committee therefore tend to see this committee as "more
equal than the rest," hardly a recipe for board wholeness. What can
become a board within the board is to be avoided.

Earlier we listed three steps in accountable delegation: First, setting expectations for performance. Second, identifying delegatees.
Third, inspecting evidence that expectations were met. At this
point, we have discussed the first two of these three steps in the delegation sequence. We can now move to the third step.

Checking to See That Expectations Have Been Met

When the board has delegated the running of the organization to
the CEO and the guiding of board process to the CGO, it needs
to check that these delegatees and the board itself did their jobs.

Indeed, setting expectations for performance and not checking that they were met could hardly be called delegation; abdication might be a more apt description. We will use the word *monitoring* to refer to the board's checking CEO and organizational performance, though *evaluation, reporting,* and *performance appraisal* would work as well. We will use the term *self-evaluation* to refer to the board's checking its own and its CGO's performance. We will look first at monitoring.

Checking Organizational Performance

Monitoring information is evaluative; it is judgmental. It seeks to discover if the CEO led the organization to the accomplishment of reasonable interpretations of Ends policies and the avoidance of the means prohibited in Executive Limitations policies, reasonably interpreted. Monitoring information is necessarily focused on the past, which is a good reason for finding an efficient way to monitor so that looking backward doesn't become a dominant board characteristic. Due to its judgmental quality, monitoring information must always be criteria-based, so that even when it is rigorous, it is still fair. Since monitoring is a comparison between what the board said it wanted or didn't want and what it actually got, it would be meaningless if the board had set no expectations in the first place.

Because the CEO's accountability is identical to the operational organization's job, monitoring CEO performance is the same as evaluation of the organization. Clearly, the continual board assessment of CEO success is too important to be carelessly done or put off. Because of its importance, we deal with monitoring the CEO's job more thoroughly in the Carver Policy Governance Guide titled *Evaluating CEO and Board Performance*. For now, we will simply point out that monitoring must include two elements: first, the disclosure of the CEO's interpretation of the policy being monitored, along with his or her rationale for the reasonableness of that interpretation; second, data that demonstrate the accomplishment, or its lack, of the interpretation. The CEO's interpretation is always decided and disclosed by the CEO, whereas the data may be gathered by the CEO, by parties under CEO authority, by parties not under CEO authority engaged by the board, and, rarely, by the board itself.

The CEO's interpretation is phrased in a measurable form, an "operational definition." No matter how unmeasurable a board policy might appear, then, it is always measurable because the reasonable interpretation must be measurable. Accomplishment of policy can therefore be evaluated both rigorously and fairly by the board, even though the board has not had to do all the complicated work of stating its expectations as measures. (This is further explained in the Guide *Evaluating CEO and Board Performance*.)

> So if you are a board member, you might find it difficult to suppress your natural personal reaction to the CEO, whether positive or negative. Just keep in mind your obligation to the ownership is that the organization works, even if that means ignoring whether you like or don't like the current CEO.

Checking Board Performance

Having strongly made the point that judgment of performance must be directly related to previously stated criteria, you will not be surprised at our saying that board self-evaluation follows the same rule. The previously stated criteria in this case are found in the board's Governance Process and Board-Management Delegation policies. We find the need for written reports to be less pressing in board self-evaluation but strongly encourage boards to use an informal way of comparing their governance to the policies about their governance on a very frequent basis. Frequency of self-evaluation will assist in the board's learning and proficiency with the Policy Governance model. (We deal more with board self-evaluation in the Carver Policy Governance Guide titled *Evaluating CEO and Board Performance*.)

The Policy Governance model described in this Guide takes some learning and a lot of discipline to get right. If you are interested in using this powerful but sometimes counterintuitive method of governance, your board's thoroughly understanding it is a must. Only then can your board establish policies that will form the framework of all ongoing work in the organization. We discuss this implementation process in considerable detail in the Carver Policy Governance Guide titled *Implementing Policy Governance and Staying on Track*.

Conclusion

In this Guide, we have provided a description of the Policy Governance model, outlining its major principles and describing the contrast between this powerful governance approach and the practices of more traditional boards. Practiced by countless boards across the world, the Policy Governance model is a challenging tool that enables boards to ensure effective, efficient, prudent, and ethical organizational performance.

About the Authors

John Carver is internationally known as the creator of the breakthrough in board leadership called the Policy Governance model and is the best-selling author of *Boards That Make a Difference* (1990, 1997, 2006). He is co-editor (with his wife, Miriam Carver) of the bimonthly periodical *Board Leadership*, author of over 180 articles published in nine countries, and author or co-author of six books. For over thirty years, he has worked internationally with governing boards, his principal practice being in the United States and Canada. Dr. Carver is an editorial review board member of *Corporate Governance: An International Review*, adjunct professor in the University of Georgia Institute for Nonprofit Organizations, and formerly adjunct professor in York University's Schulich School of Business.

Miriam Carver is a Policy Governance author and consultant. She has authored or co-authored over forty articles on the Policy Governance model and co-authored three books, including *Reinventing Your Board* and *The Board Member's Playbook*. She has worked with the boards of nonprofit, corporate, governmental, and cooperative organizations on four continents. Ms. Carver is the co-editor of the bimonthly periodical *Board Leadership* and, with John Carver, trains consultants in the theory and implementation of Policy Governance in the Policy Governance Academy.

John Carver can be reached at P. O. Box 13007, Atlanta, Georgia 30324-0007. Phone 404-728-9444; email johncarver@carvergovernance.com.

Miriam Carver can be reached at P. O. Box 13849, Atlanta, Georgia 30324-0849. Phone 404-728-0091; email miriamcarver@carvergovernance.com.